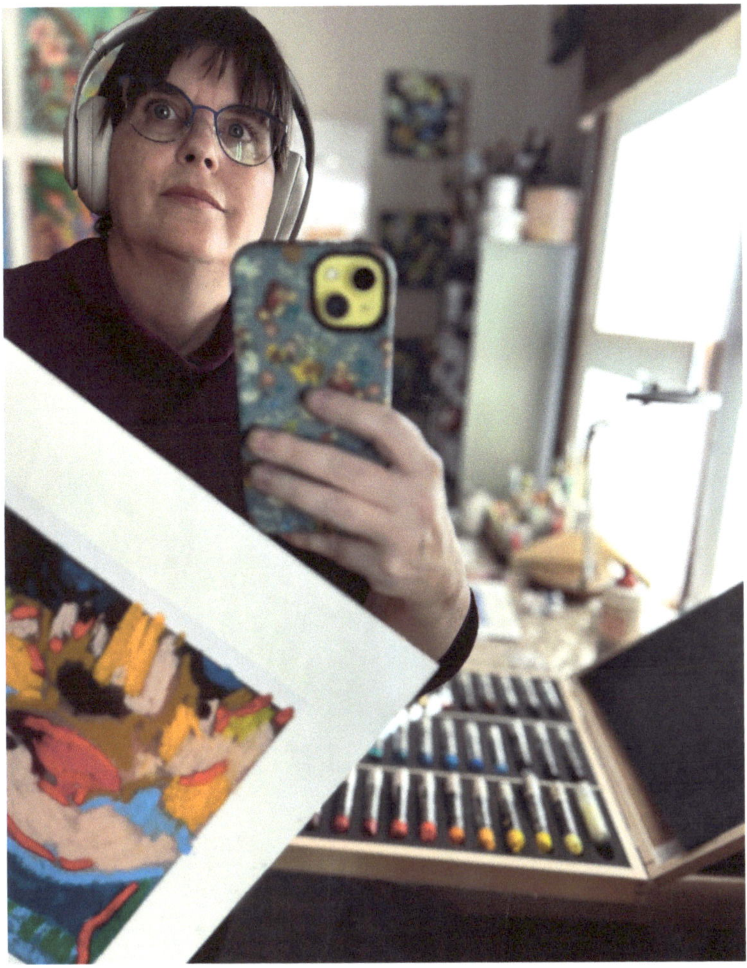

# UNMASKED MEMORIES
Paintings and Haikus
by Angela Meijer

I DREAM OF PAINTING
AND THEN I PAINT
MY DREAM.

- VINCENT VAN GOGH

# Attic Dream

I went up the ladder into my grandparent's attic. There was a window in the roof that let light into the attic. There was also a small table with a chair sitting in the space with the other storage. On the table was a large book, opened about halfway through the book. When I sat at the table, I knew it was a book of my life. It was in black and white, but as I looked at the page, it began to fill with color, and the color started traveling backward in time and bringing color into previous pages; it was also getting more color into future pages. As I would open up pages of my memories, they began to fill up with color, which would also travel into the coming pages and, at the same time, into the pages of the past.

I woke up from my dream and knew that as I looked at my memories with kindness, color would heal them and change my perspective moving forward.

Recently, I've been developing personal work. I'm usually very private about the portraits I make, and I rarely share them. However, when I paint myself, I can process things in a way that reveals thought patterns that I often cannot cognate otherwise. I scanned old negatives of self-portraits throughout the years and started painting them with oil sticks. I realized I was revisiting my memories with color as I did in my attic dream. I've also been painting imagined gardens that represent growth in my life, and I've been focusing on the language of flowers. I pasted prints of my face from archived photographs in these two paintings and worked myself into these imagined gardens. One is of me as a gardener by day, and the other is me enveloped by a garden in my dreams.

*She plants her desires developing her voice she Dares sing a new song.*

**The Gardener**

acrylic, collage and oil stick on canvas
24x30 inches.

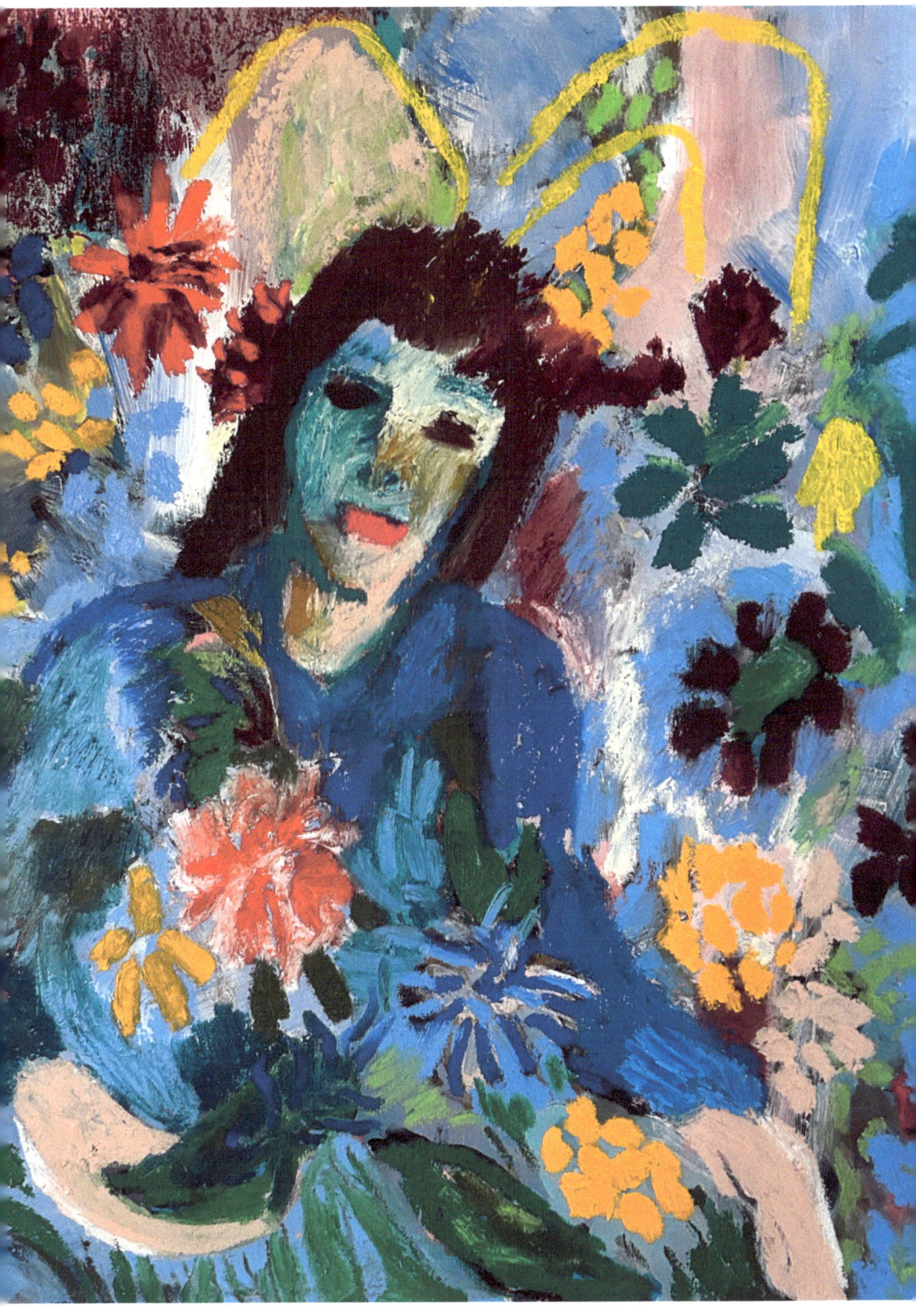

Breathing in deeply
    Forbidding Regret exhales
Up comes the Vista

**Breath of Life**

acrylic, collage and oil stick on canvas
24x30 inches.

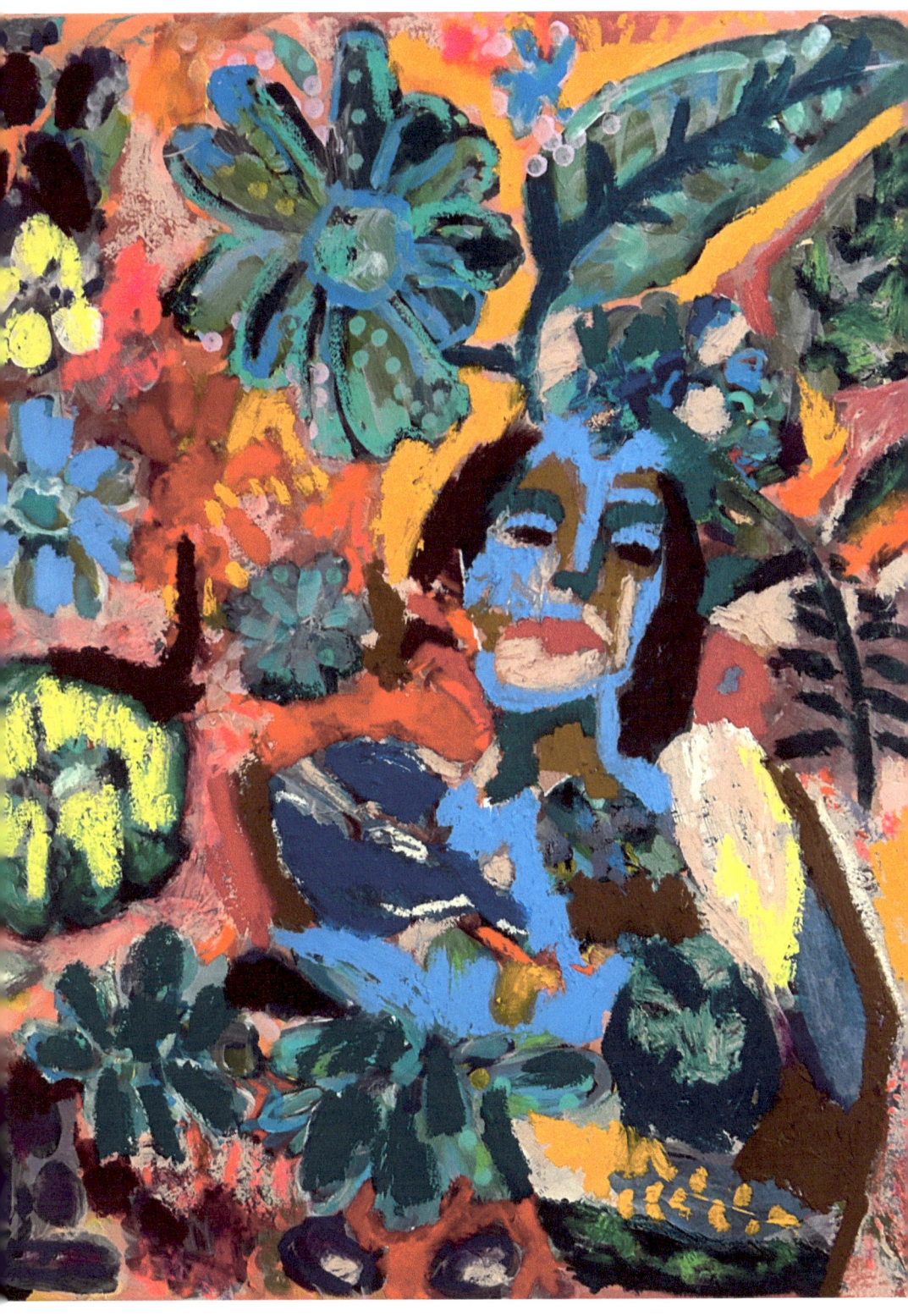

*Your Spirit is Near
Songs emerge from the blues
Dancing in Neon.*

**Hummingbird Floral Symphonies**

oil stick and pigment inks on paper
12x16 inches

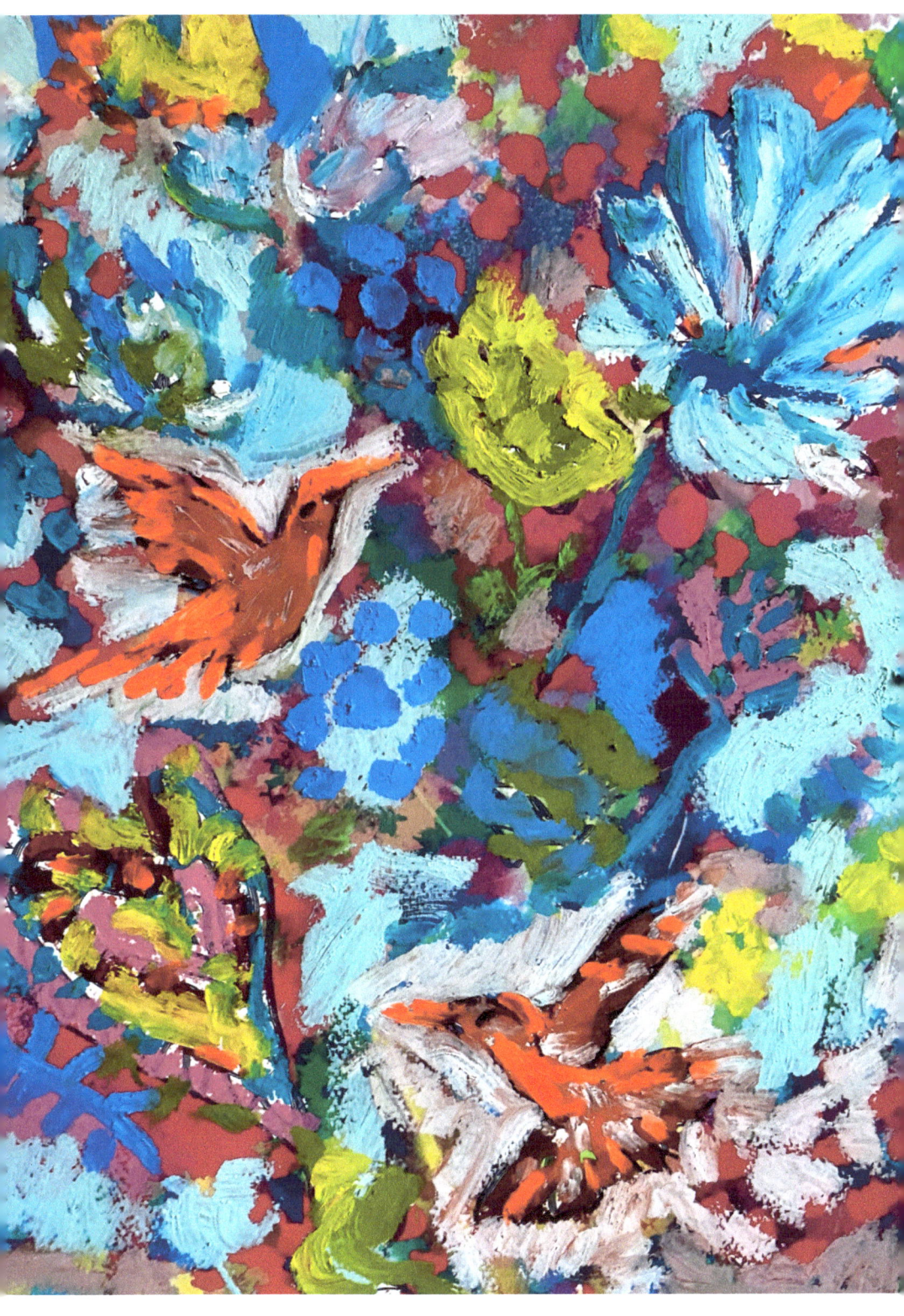

Strokes of Bright-Pigment
hovers Flourescent Verdant
water and Sunshine

**Honeybees Floral Symphonies**

oil stick and pigment inks on paper
12x16 inches

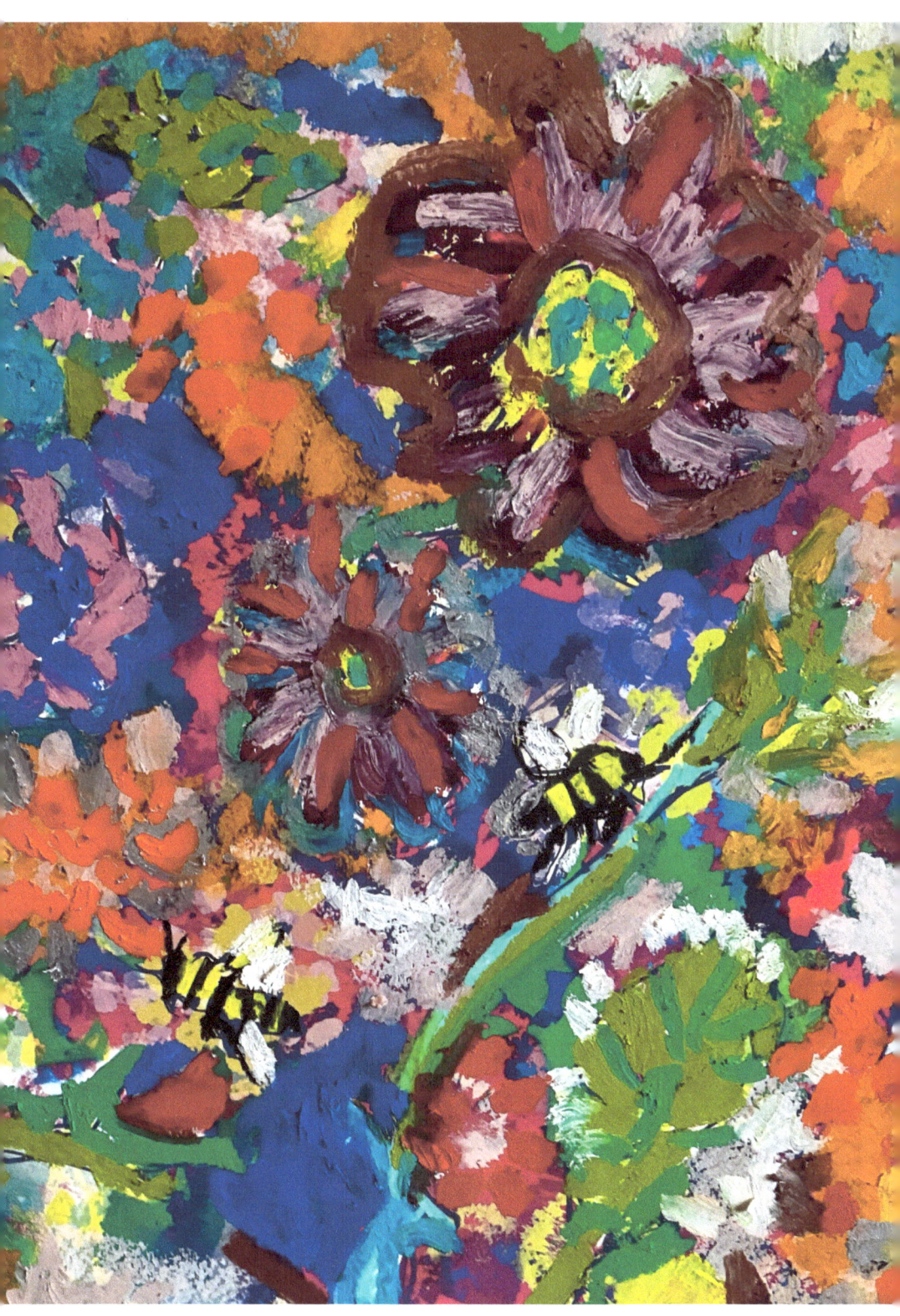

*Protect and Shield me*
*Ladybird carry my hope*
*Waking the Dawn*

**Ladybugs Floral Symphonies**

oil stick and pigment inks on paper
12x16 inches

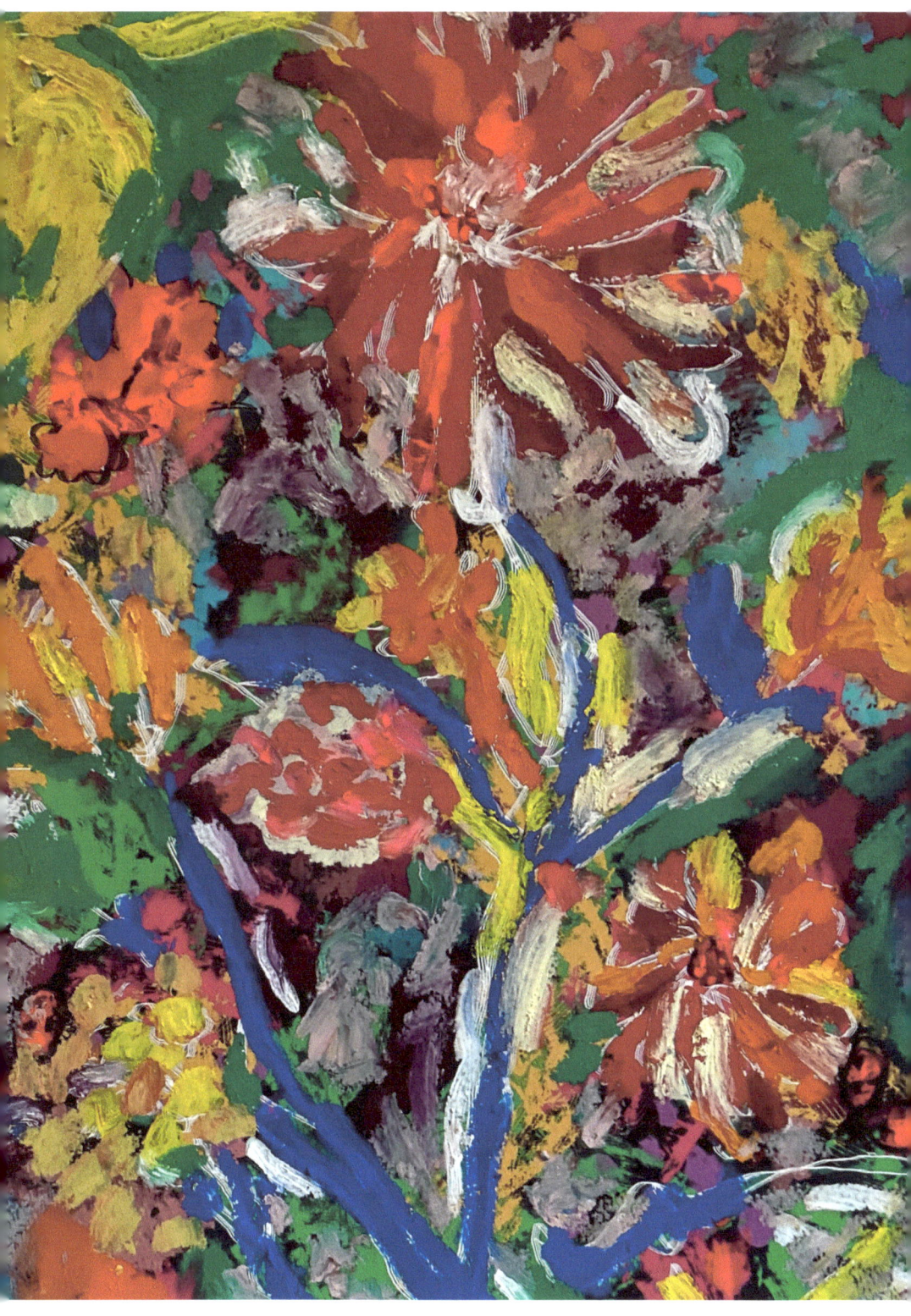

*Red as in Glowing*
*Take up all the Room you need*
*Evolve and fly light*

**Butterflies Floral Symphonies**

oil stick and pigment inks on paper
12x16 inches

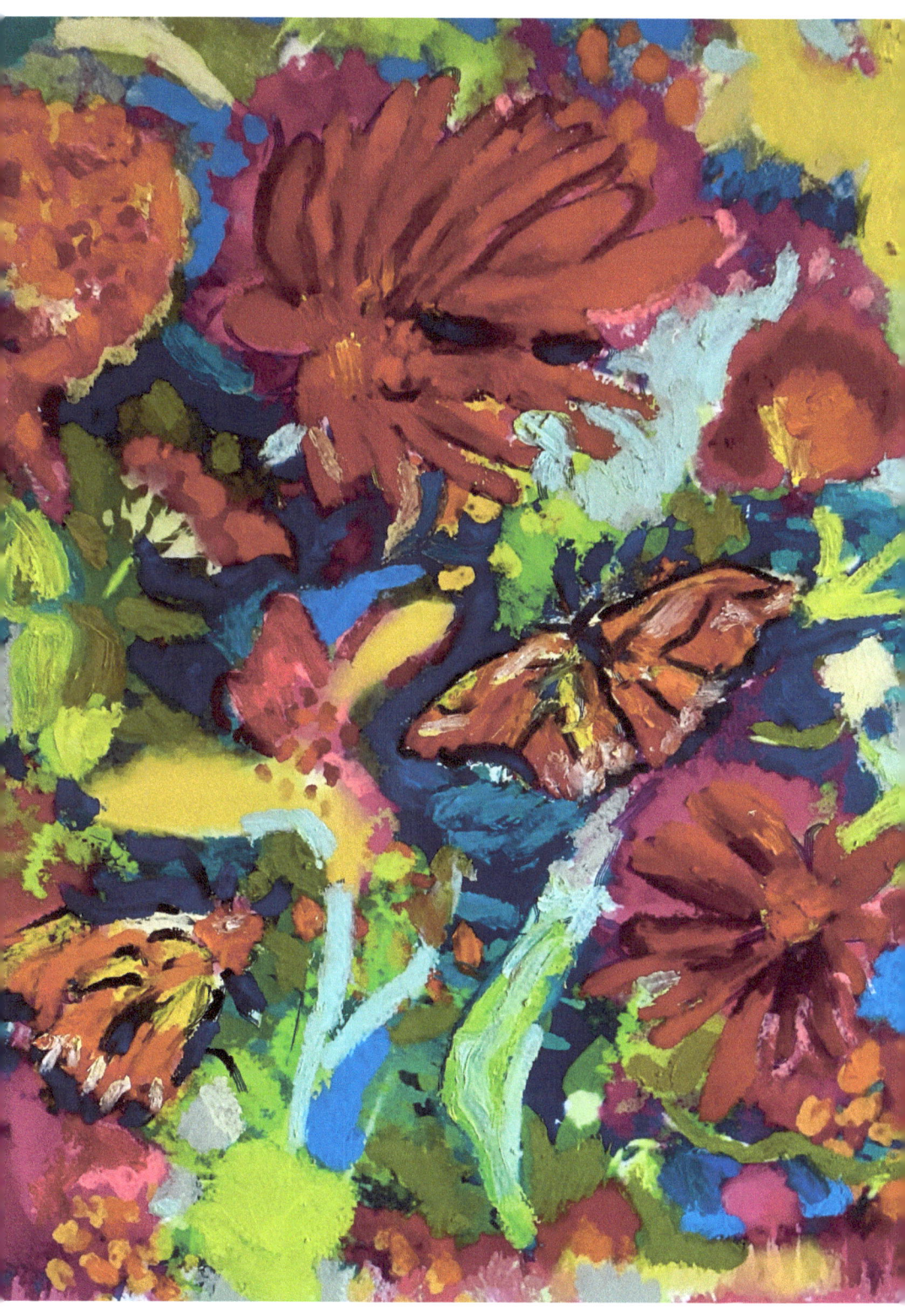

*How do I face this?*
*Will I repeat history?*
*Watch me take a stand.*

**Echoed Bravery**

oil stick on photograph
8x10 inches

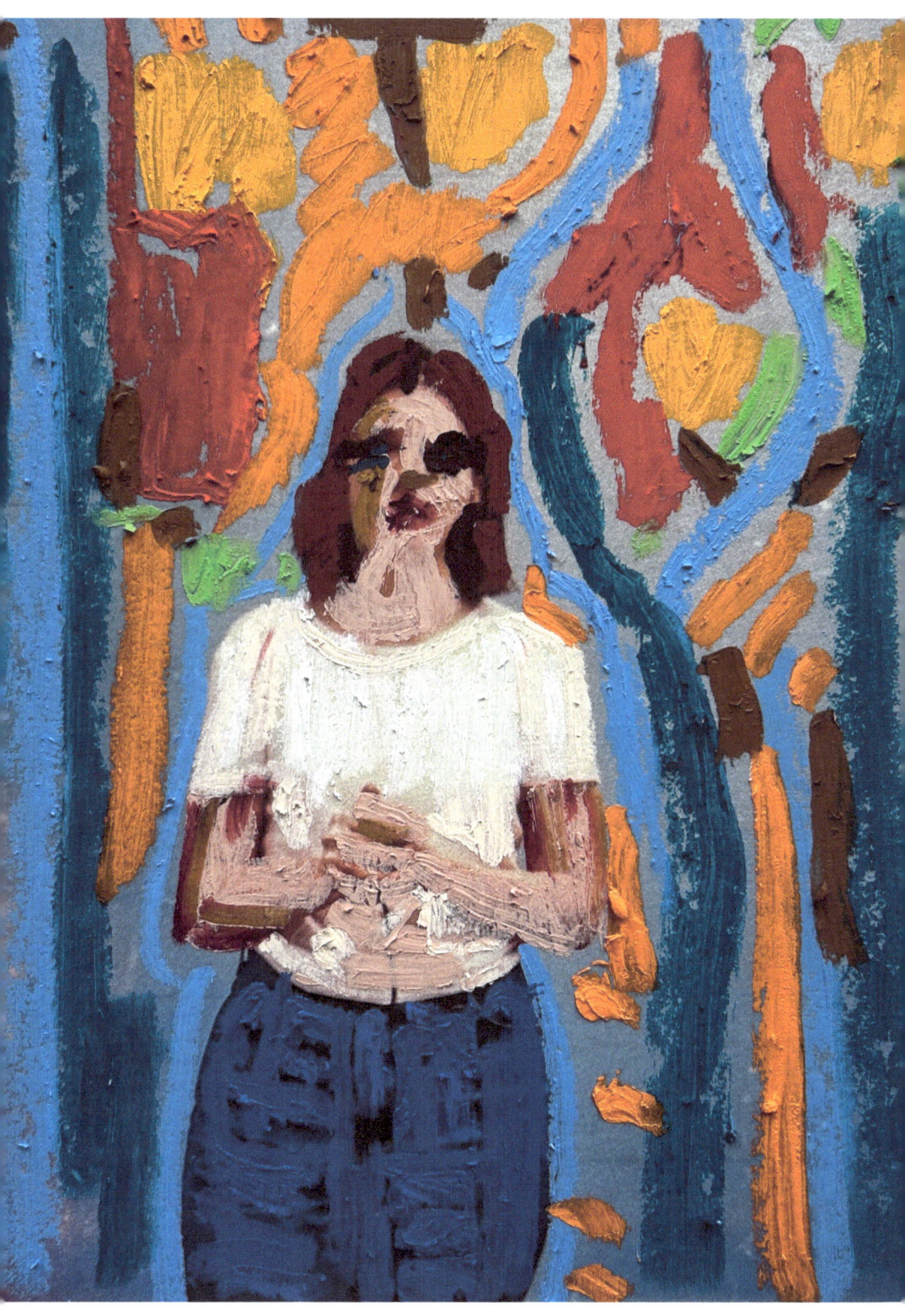

Remorse can sit down
As I look to my future
Kick fear in the head.

**Memories Reimagined**

oil stick on photograph
8x10 inches

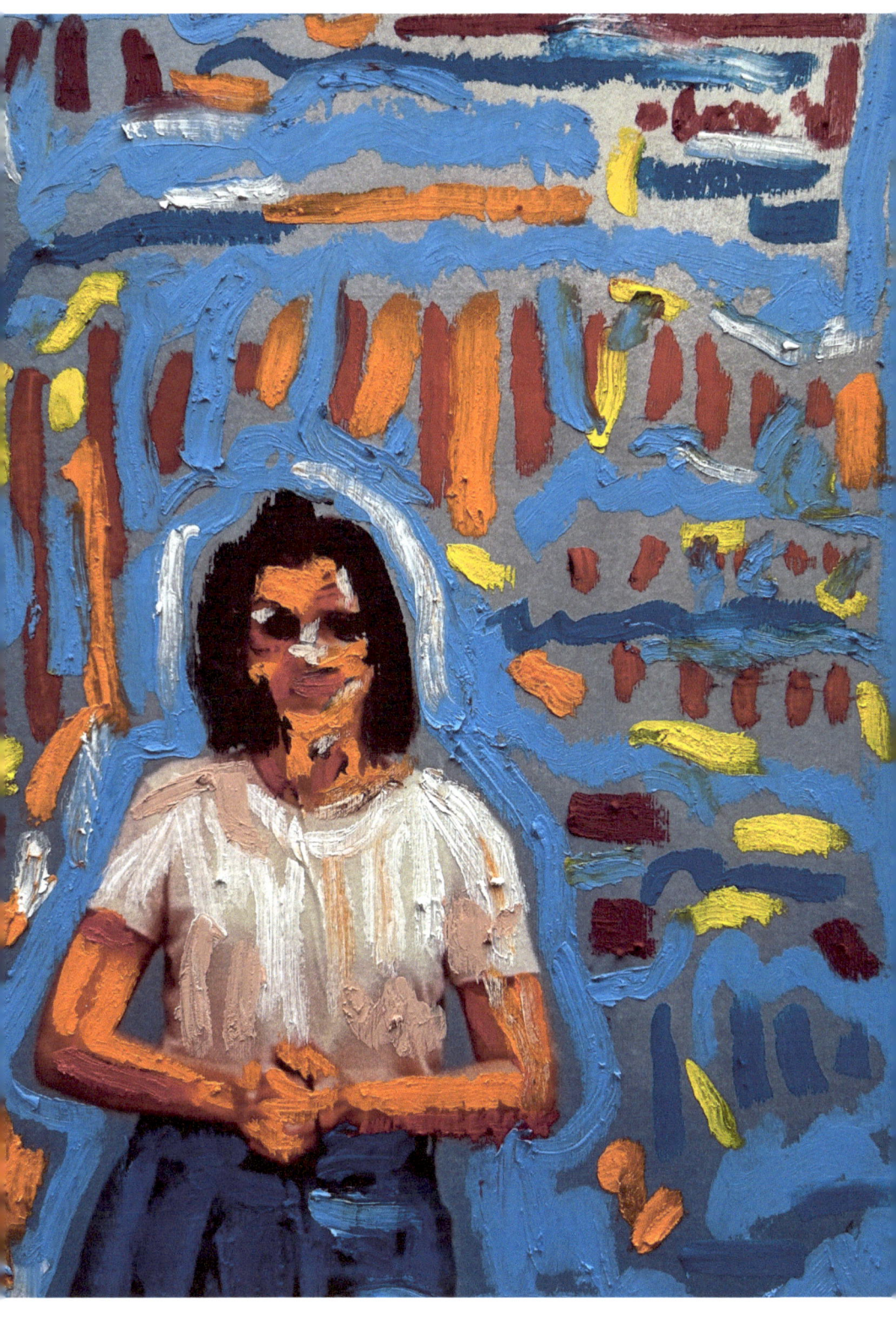

Now I am happy
Yellow and Red tulips fill
Dutch gray skies with blue.

**Reclaimed Past**
oil stick on photograph

8x10 inches

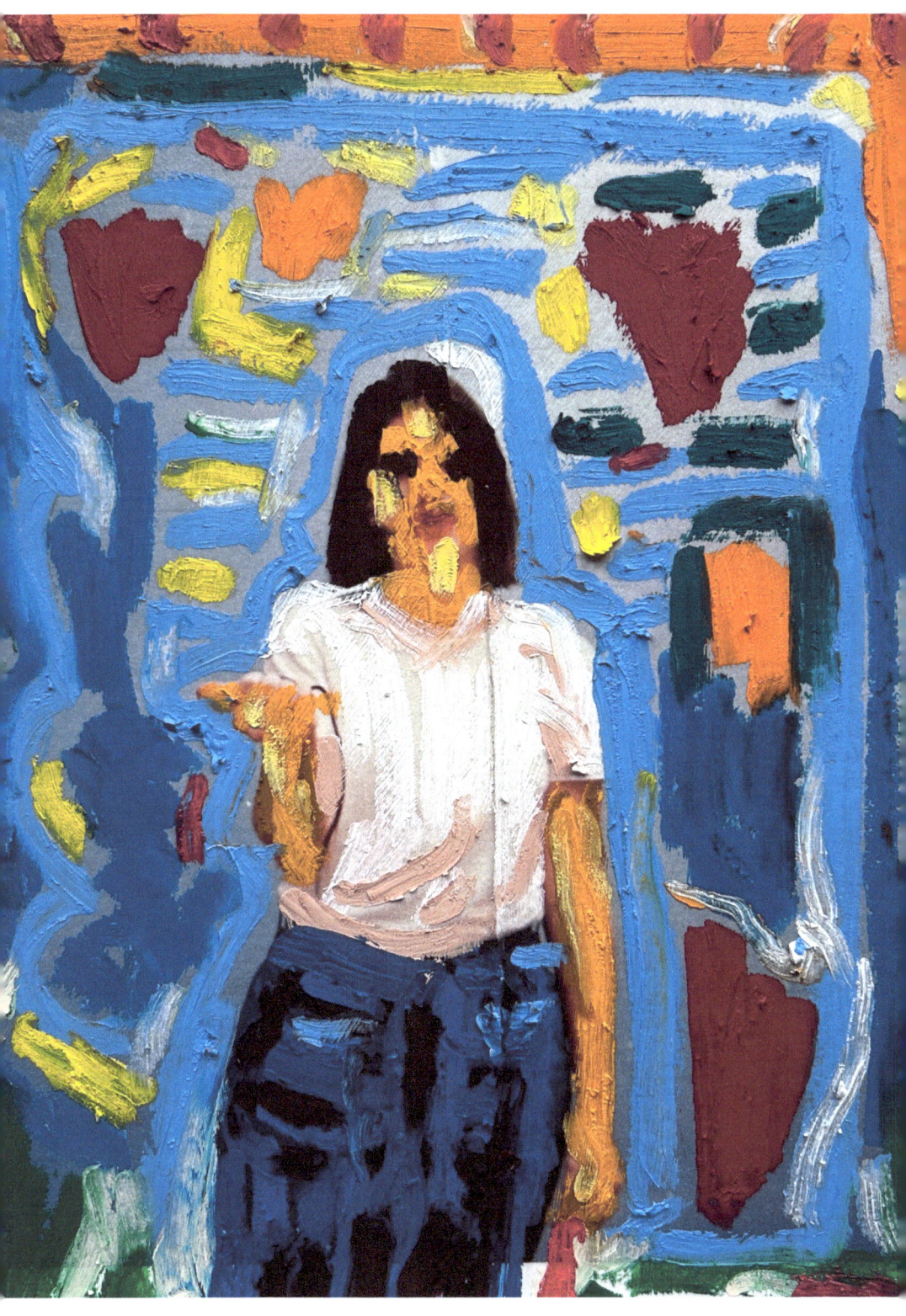

Passion and Desire
can sometimes overshadow
My heart will stay pure

**Strength Strokes**

oil stick on photograph
8x10 inches

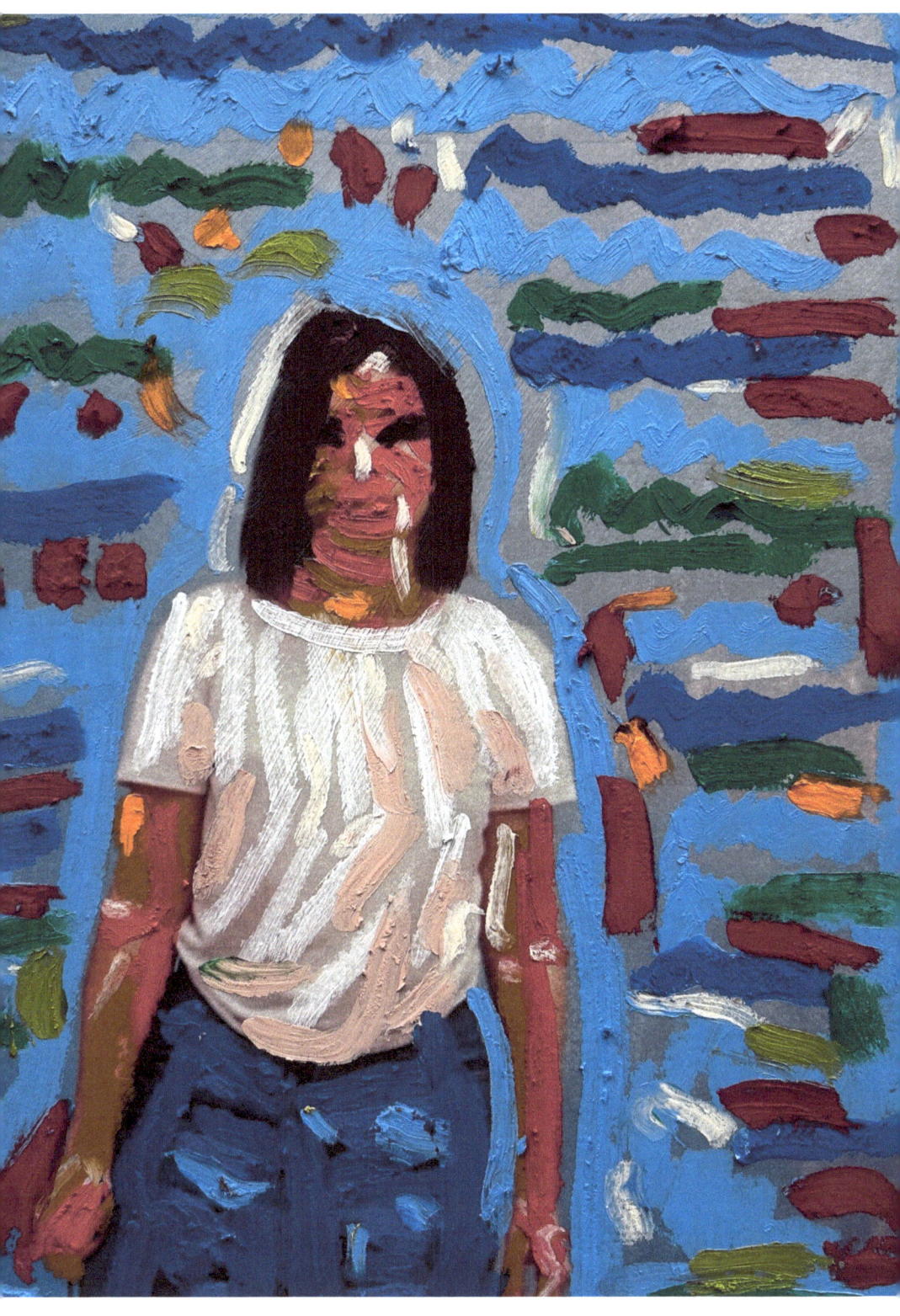

My eyes are closed now
I still see on the inside
Take a deep breath now.

**Bold Revisions**

oil stick on photograph
8x8 inches

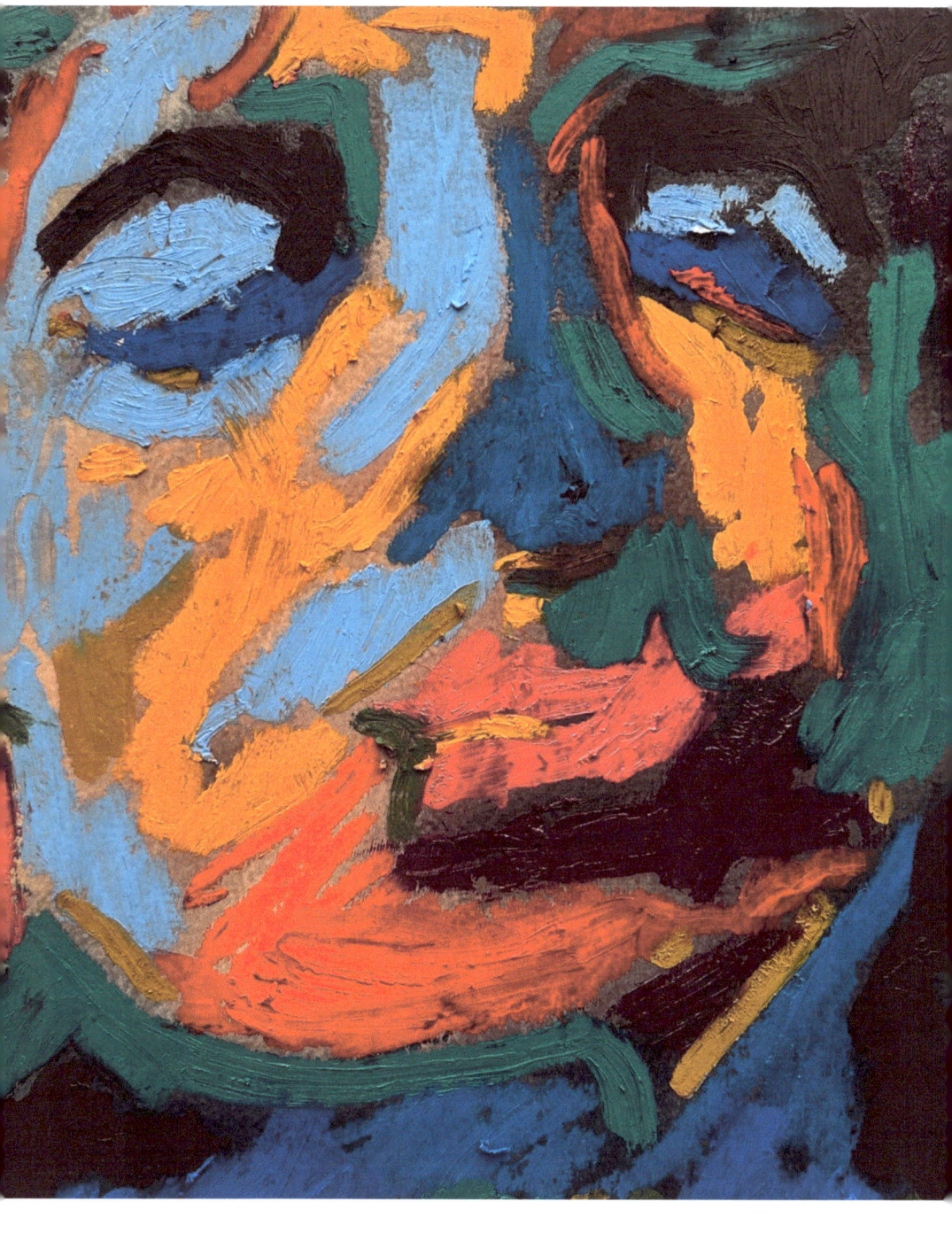

*Years later I see what I thought was self pity was the strength to feel.*

**Transformed Shadows**

oil stick on photograph
8x10 inches

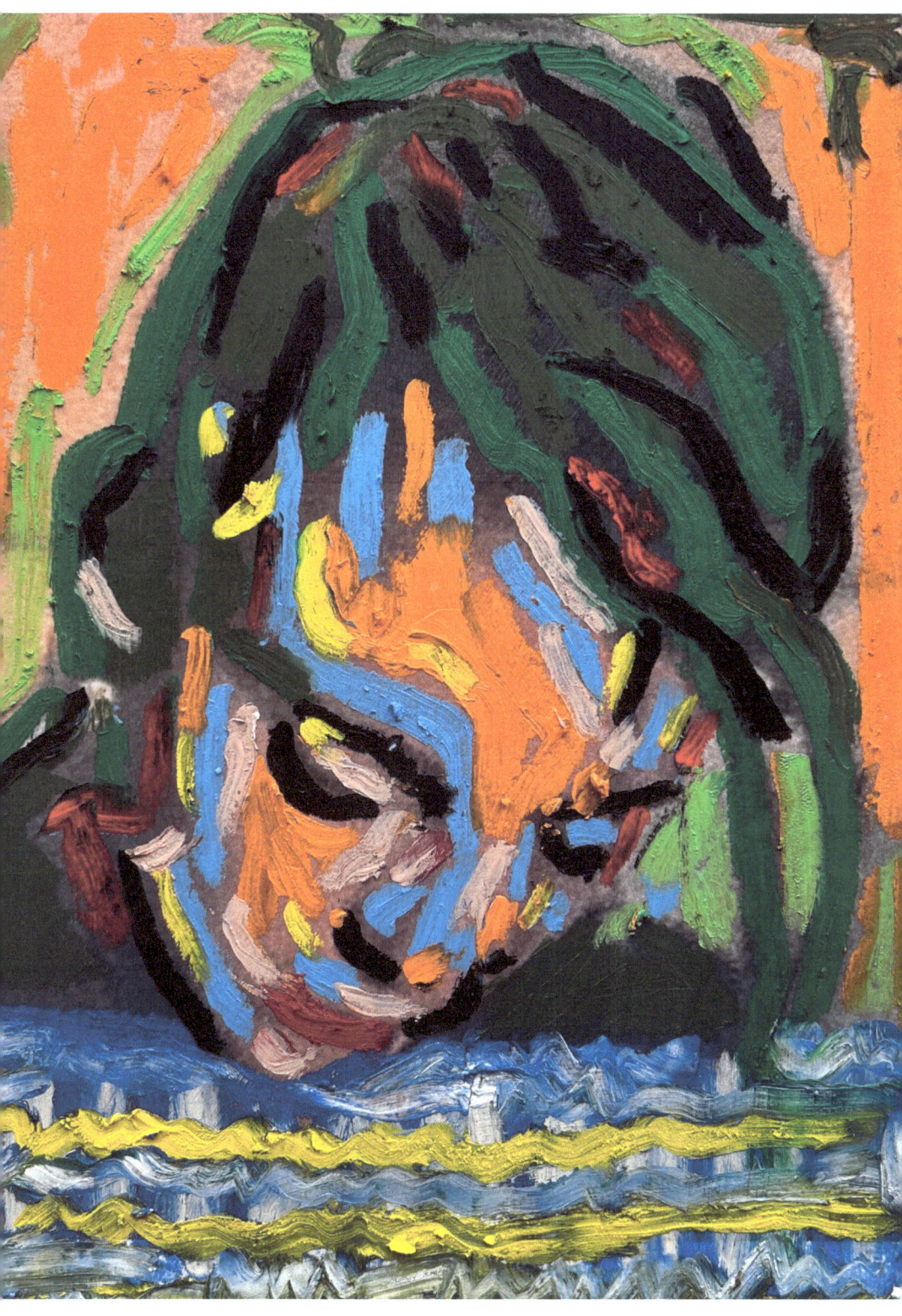

*My heart is tender
Oh God have mercy on Us.
let us love better.*

**Brave Palette**

oil stick on photograph
8x10 inches

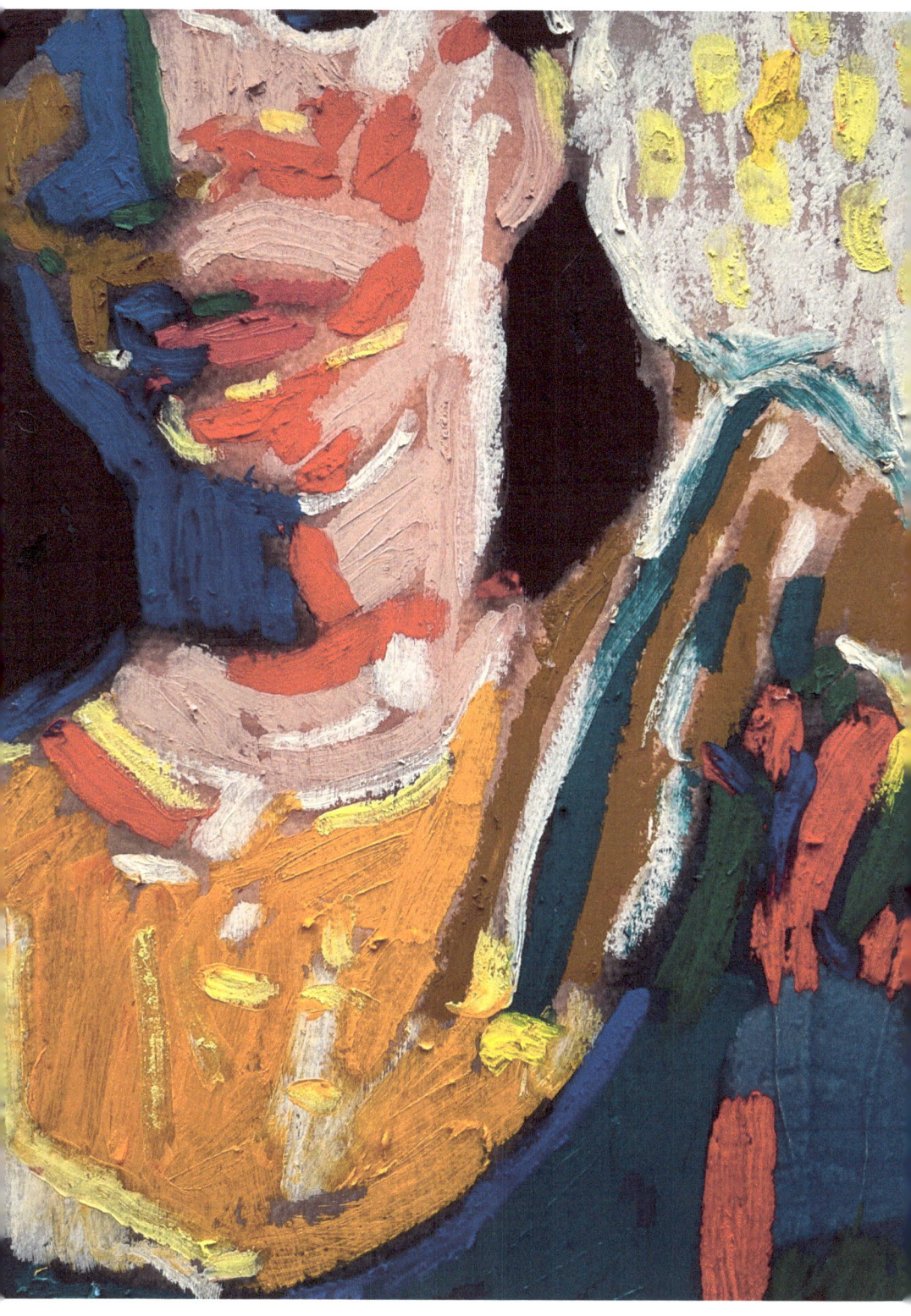

*Oh eyes be kinder
Remember your thoughts create
how you will see things*

**Vivid Reflections**

oil stick on photograph
8x10 inches

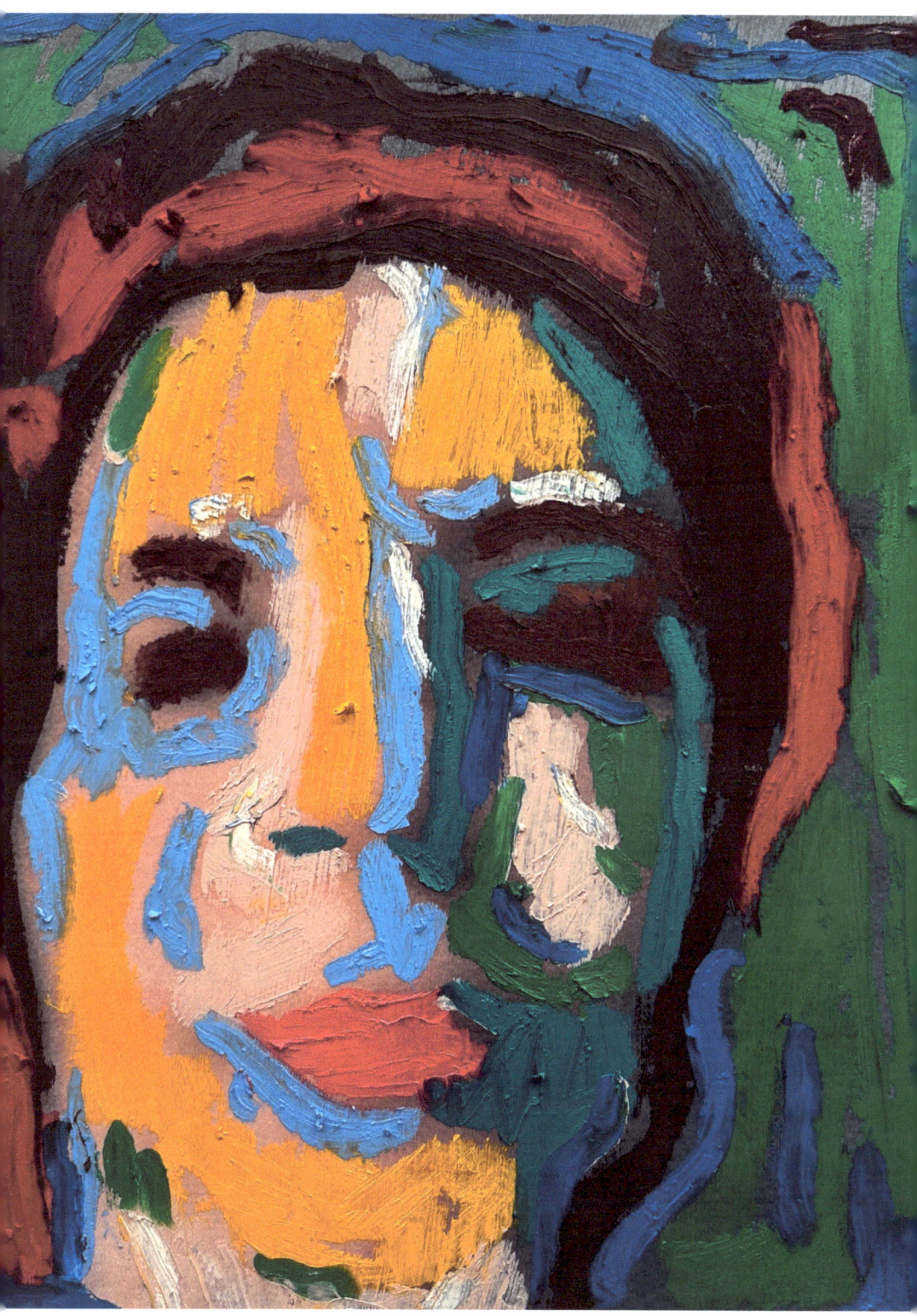

*I hung my shame up*
*So everyone could see it*
*Now It can not rule*

**Unmasked Memory**

oil stick on photograph
8x8 inches

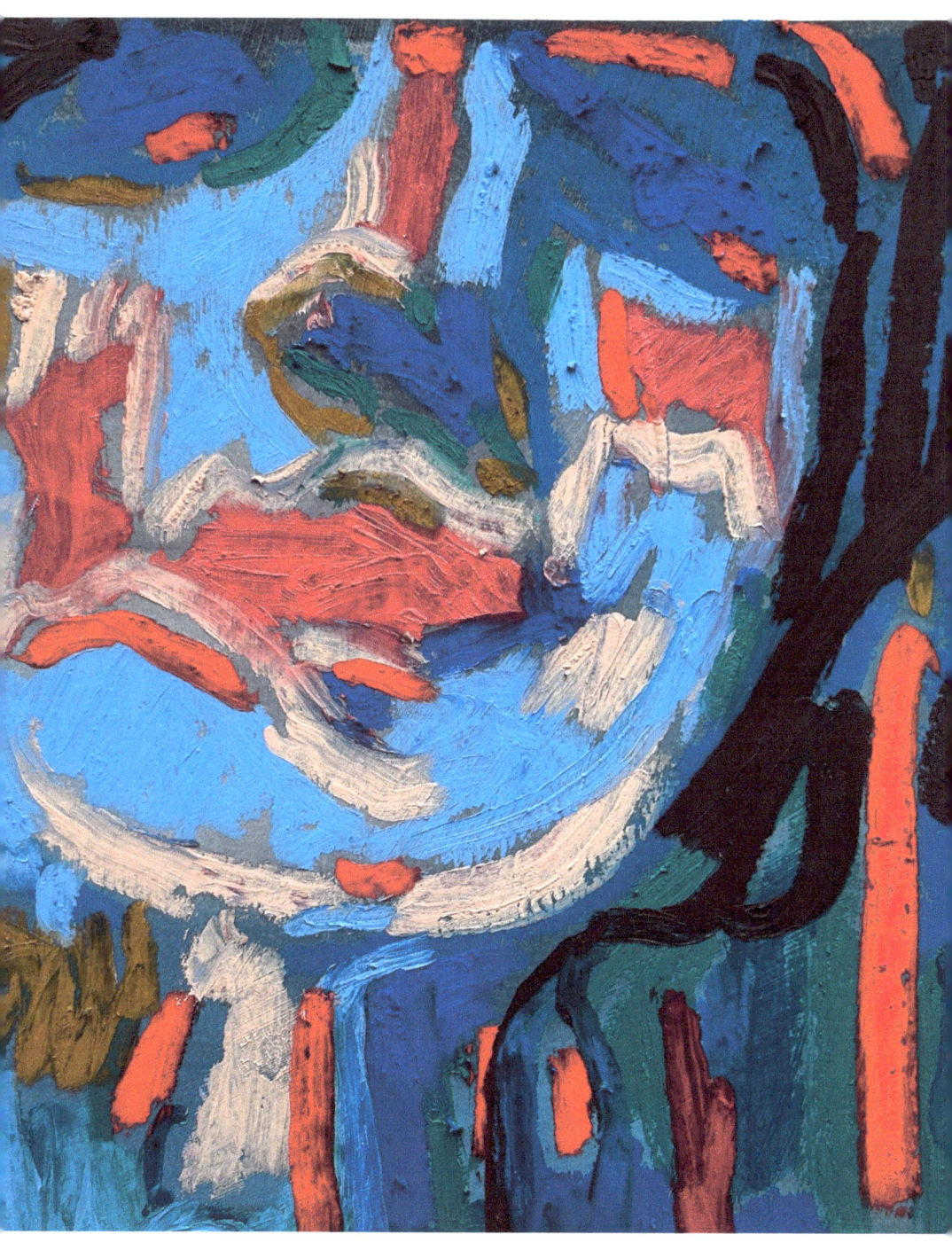

Limited Palette
   doesn't carry this message
wear it Declare it

**Chromatic Bravery**

oil stick on photograph
8x10 inches

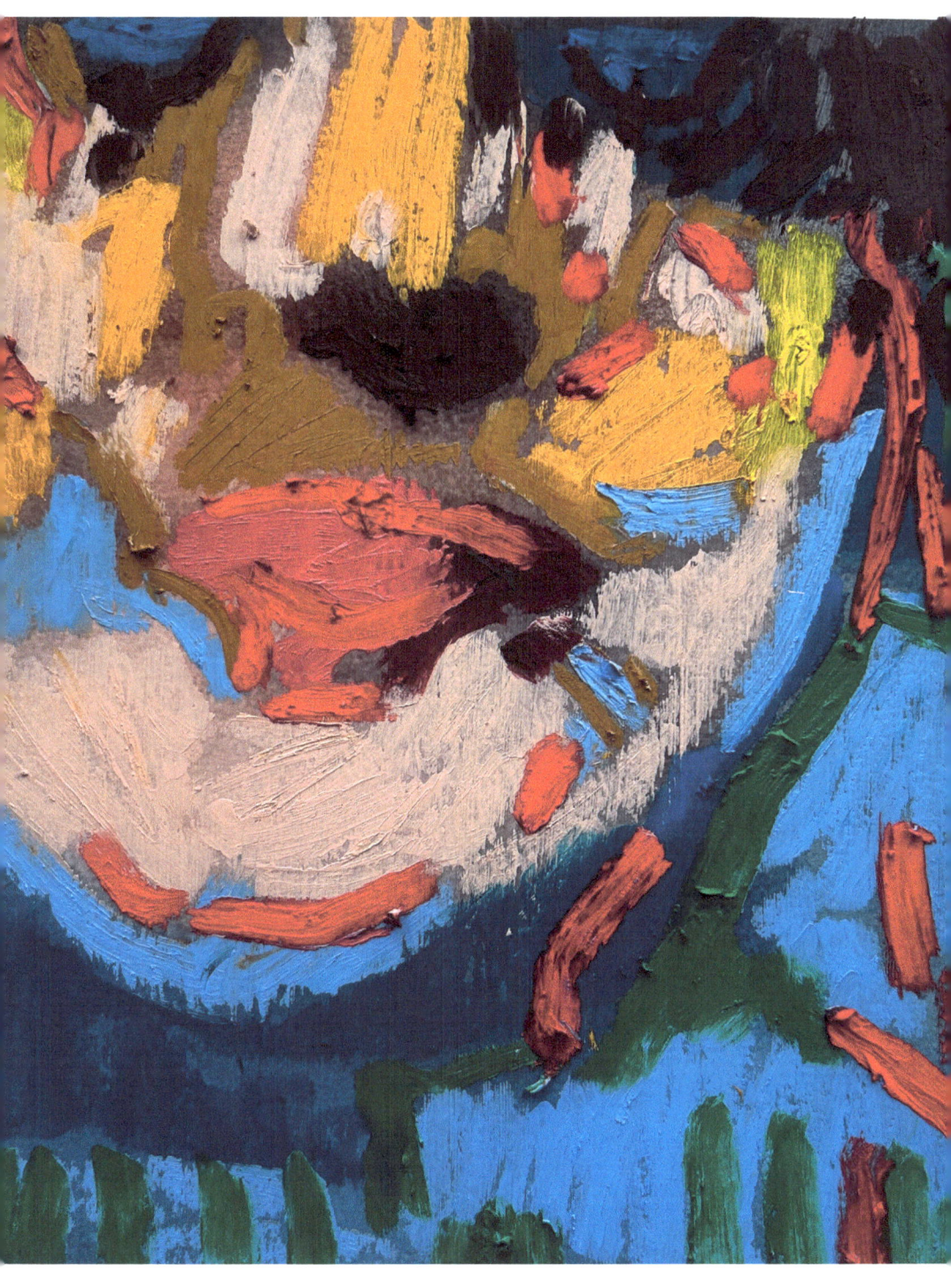

Atrophy choked me
Now the brain fog has lifted
I'm breathing again.

**Fearless Reflections**

oil stick on photograph
8x10 inches

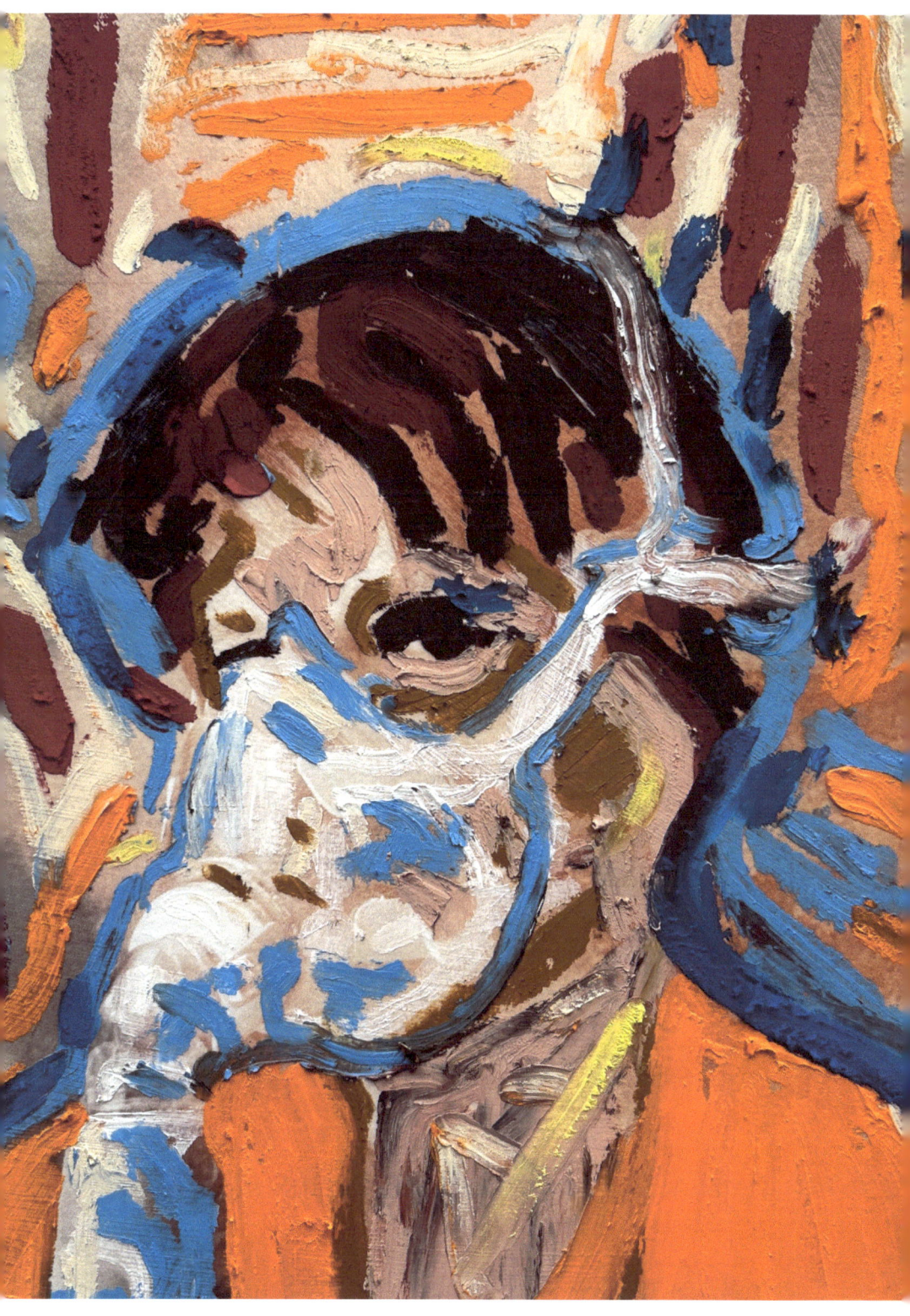

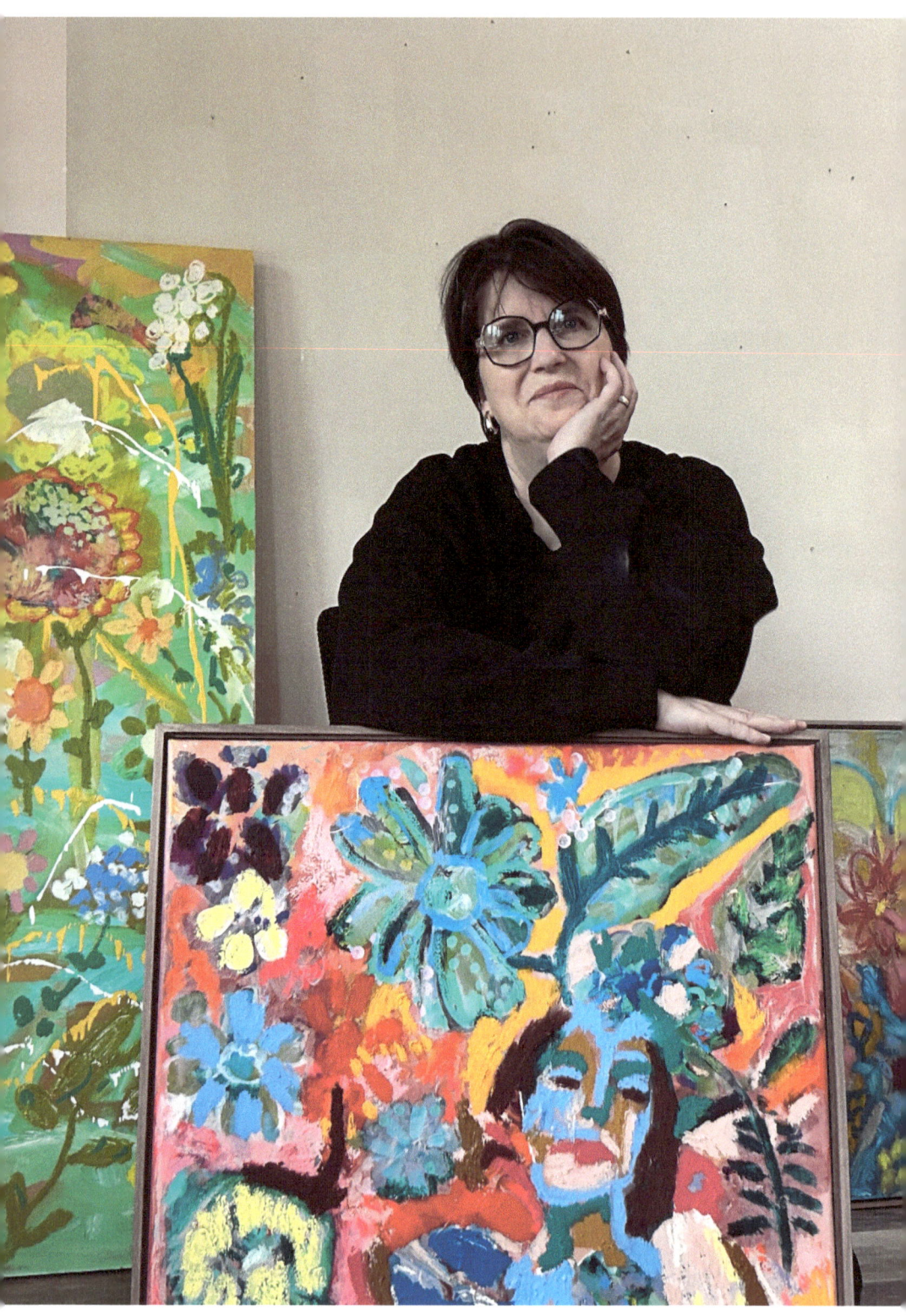

# Artist Bio

Meijer graduated with a BFA in fine art photography nearly 30 years ago, and has been exploring visual language ever since. Her photography can be found in International collections and publications. Twenty years ago, Angela traded in her camera, invested in paints and canvases, and started painting daily from the inside out. Her artwork was primarily abstract and nonrepresentational until a few years ago. Many of these paintings are in private and corporate collections. In 2021, Angela invested in a camera and started photographing and painting flowers. Her current artwork is inspired by the language of flowers.

In "Unmasked Memories," Meijer layers vivid color over self-portrait photographs and creates collages within abstract, Fauvist-inspired gardens. Inspired by how memories shift over time, her work invites viewers to consider how perception and emotion influence personal history.

You can find Angela Meijer's artwork at:
www.angelameijer.com

© Angela Meijer. 2024. All Rights Reserved.

www.ingramcontent.com/pod-product-compliance
Lightning Source LLC
Chambersburg PA
CBHW040338220526
45473CB00009B/2727